HOW TO ANALYZE PEOPLE

A Psychologist's Guide to Master the Art of Speed Reading Anyone, Through Psychological Techniques & Body Language Analysis

KATHERINE CHAMBERS

TABLE OF CONTENTS

INTRODUCTION

"People may not always tell you how they feel about you, but they will always show you. Pay attention"

(Avinash Wandre)

Psychology is such a fascinating subject as it deals with the very thing humans find most interesting, ourselves. It deals with the ways in which we interact with the world around us, and the other people in it. I believe this is the reason I spent so much of my early adult life studying the academic side of the various psychological principles.

I continually get asked questions regarding certain mental tendencies, especially when it comes to analyzing themselves, and of course the other people around them. People are always astonished by the accuracy of what I'm telling them, when in reality all I am doing is simply pointing out obvious human tendencies which everyone can see. I just direct their focus back towards it.

The follow up question is then almost always the same I.e. "Do you analyze everyone you meet? Are you analyzing me now?" I never miss the opportunity to pretend that I have picked up some deep and dark secret the person has been hiding away. The momentary look of panic and shock on their face is too priceless to pass up!

However the reality is, not all psychologists are assessing everyone, all of the time. Of course we do in certain situations which would benefit us most. Or within clinical settings for instance. But you wouldn't expect a driving instructor to be assessing every driver on the road. Or an architect to survey every building they walk into.

Analyzing people is no different. You do it when you are required to do it. I have to be honest though. Once you open your eyes to some of the techniques and strategies I will teach in the following chapters, you may find yourself picking up on these tendencies a lot more quickly, and without realizing you have done so. After all, human behavior is the most predictable thing on the planet. When you know what you are looking for.

I liken it to a scene in the first Jason Bourne movie, where Matt Damon is sitting in a cafe still rather confused about who he is and what he has done in the past. However for reasons unknown to him, he can recall every car registration plate in the parking lot, has sized up all of the males in the room and knows the location of every exit.

Analyzing human behavior and body language is very similar. It's about effortlessly and automatically picking up on the subtle movements and gestures of others, the unconscious mannerisms they themselves are unaware of making.

Of course you need to start out with what a person is saying. The words they are choosing to use. However this is only the tip of the iceberg in the people reading game. Words can mask intention, but body language will always reveal a persons true thinking. It will shine a light on their deeper thoughts, feelings and emotions.

In reality, successfully analyzing others is about doing two things in any situation:

1. Accurately assessing contextual cues, the character/culture and situational elements which are likely to dictate the way people are behaving.

2. Spotting "in the moment" body language signals or "tells" which give away true motive and intention.

My aim for this book is to lay out these overarching contextual principles first and foremost, to give you the grounding and a framework of reference to work with. But to also give you a look into your own behavior and psychology, to provide an insight to why people behave in the ways they do. But ultimately give you the tools and practical strategies for speed reading anyone in your daily life. So get ready for your new super power.

My Credentials

Before we get into the ins and outs of analyzing others, it's probably a good idea for me to explain exactly who I am, and why you should even bother listening to me in the first place. Yes I have the undergraduate and master's degree in psychology from Stanford, but my main focus over the past 15 years or so has been on the practical elements of the discipline. I wouldn't ever call myself a "Self-Help Guru" but I do focus much more on the results of these principles in the real world compared to my previous life of studying endless research papers on the academic side of the subject.

I use what I have learned and observe the behavior and psychological patterns of other successful people in life to pin point exactly what it is they are doing to elicit the results they are achieving. There are common patterns to these people and behaviors if you know how to spot them. Fortunately for you even if you don't, I have spent the past 2 decades working this stuff out for you. I have dedicated my 40's to documenting both the rationale behind the most important psychological mindsets as well as the practical advice on how to cultivate the ability to use them to your benefit in the real world.

It all started when I was just a young girl growing up on the east coast, I was a very observant kid. I was the youngest of four in our family which was fine with me as I would get to watch my older sister and brothers in action. Watch for their actions and behaviors, their successes and failures as almost a dry run for what I should be doing.

This continued through high school and into college, I had a very active and ambitious peer group, it's hard not to when you live on the Stanford campus. I played a high level of lacrosse as well as track and field whilst at university so got to view the psychology of team/individual sports as well as in academia.

However it's not since leaving college life and living in the real world that I have really developed a taste for the subjects I once studied. It's all well and good reading the intricacies of psychological theories from the comfort of your dorm room or library, but it's not until you have to put these theories to the test in life in general do you really understand how they work. It's not until you have to make your way in business, within a career, build a family for yourself do you really understand the impact your mindset has to your overall success.

For me that has been building a multi-six figure consulting business and now a family of my own. But I am not here to blow my own horn or preach in anyway, nobody needs that. What I will do is put things into perspective, what I know to be true from the science behind these principles combined with my experience in the real world. I have made many mistakes along the way and will point out these pitfalls for you.

So why am I such an expert on analyzing people? As I mentioned, I studied a wide range of topics within the field of psychology and neuroscience whilst at college, which formed my base understanding. But I have since picked up many critical skill sets whilst building a family and career of my own. Everything from managing my personal and business relationships to my own mental state. Everything has been a learning curve and one which has taken deep emotional understanding and soul searching at times.

The real world is about problem solving, it's about rapport building and getting the most out of the interactions you have. It's about discerning the true intentions of others so you do not waste time with individuals who say one thing, but do another. Life is too short for that. If I can show you how to better assess potential business partners, romantic mates or simply strangers on the street. Then I have done my job.

So now that you know a little more about me, let's dive in. The following chapters will teach you everything you need to know in order to become proficient at spotting human verbal and non-verbal behavior signals. To ultimately provide you with the tools and knowledge on how to analyze anyone.

PART 1: ANALYZING PEOPLE - BODY LANGUAGE BASICS

CHAPTER 1

KNOW YOURSELF - KNOW OTHERS

"Your body communicates as well as your mouth. Don't contradict yourself"

(Allen Ruddock)

Before diving straight into the practical strategies and techniques for successfully reading and analyzing others around you, it's important to take a look at exactly why and how the body exhibits certain behaviors and reacts in the way it does in the first place.

Reading others is certainly not an exact science, but if you can understand the base psychological and physiological processes behind human body language, you can much more reliably spot them we they do arise. This will ultimately give you a distinct advantage in knowing what the other person is thinking. But it starts with you.

The following passage is an adaptation of a section within *"Emotional Intelligence: A Psychologist's Guide"* from a chapter called "Living our Limbic Legacy." It's included to illustrate the various factors within the human body and brain which have such a determining effect on the way we behave.

Nature Vs. Nurture

It's typically very difficult to convincingly or definitively settle a nature vs. nurture debate in favor of one over the other when it comes to human psychology and behavior. Knowing exactly how much of our behavior is derived from our genetics (from our parents and ancestors) and what is acquired through our environmental influences, can be a tough causal link to substantiate either way. However it's certainly an interesting question to pose especially with regards to analyzing people.

Non-verbal communication in humans is undoubtedly part of our evolutionary make-up along with the rest of our anatomical and behavioral traits. It's really just a case of deciphering exactly how much of our body language behaviors are genetically inherited and how much can be attributed to environmental influences. Darwin certainly believed that humans shared common facial expressions from birth due to an extrapolation from his findings of expressions and emotions within the animal kingdom.

These universal facial expressions comprised of happiness, sadness, fear, disgust, surprise and anger. Other researchers including

American psychologist Paul Ekman further supported this theory with his 1969 study on conversational non-verbal signals showing that there was a consistent emotional facial recognition ability of humans across a diverse cultural background.

However the genetic links become a little more tenuous when it comes to gestures, especially less fundamental and larger physical movements of the hands/arms etc which is more accurately described as kinesics. This is also true of winking of the eyes or proxemics, the technical term for the considerations of personal space. These factors seem to be much more dependent on environment, upbringing, culture and societal groups in general.

But it is certainly safe to assume that human body language behaviors are in part built into our nature I.e. inherited, and in part nurtured from our experiences I.e. learned. It seems as though the unconscious and subtle gestures such as facial expressions are born into us, whereas the broader and more pronounced physical and conscious movements/postures are largely learned behaviors picked up from the significant others around us.

The Old Mammalian Brain

However what isn't in doubt is the development and influence of the limbic system on both our physiological (appearance) and psychological (behaviors) when it comes to the non-verbal body language changes brought about by human interaction. You have to take a good look inside of yourself to realize just how much so.

The limbic system isn't a single structure within the brain but rather a set of structures which are located on both sides of the thalamus and positioned just below the cerebrum. It is sometimes referred to as the paleomammalian cortex or the "old mammalian brain" owing to the time period in which it evolved within us. Essentially these were the first structures that set us apart from our reptilian ancestors, an addition and upgrade of hardware to the primitive structures of the archipallium which is comprised of the brain stem, medulla, cerebellum and oldest basal nuclei. These structures are primarily concerned with just the base sensory organs and simple motor functions, the starting point of any complex organism.

But the limbic system can do much more than this, as a system it supports a host of other functions including emotional regulation, long-term memory capability, ambition and all types of motivational behavior in general. It is basically the driving seat of our emotion center, as the structures heavily influence the endocrine system which intern regulates the dopermaneric pleasure responses to natural and recreational highs alike.

The limbic system also has heavy input on the autonomic nervous system which mediates the "fight or flight" response within us which as we will see later on, can have many knock-on effects to human body language. However all of these elements are still very base and primitive components with regards to the human biological make-up, but which still affect our day-to-day lives in a big way even today.

As much as we try to escape this ancestral legacy with the development of the outer neocortexs which provides the machinery that primes us for complex decision making cognition. We are constantly held back by an undersized prefrontal lobe and over powering limbic system. Don't get me wrong, I would certainly rather live in a world that allowed for the emotions of love, connection and compassion which the limbic system affords, but the flip side of that is fear, jealously and aggression which is elicited from these primal centers in exactly the same way.

Now you might be wondering exactly how this affects our body language and the answer is in a monumental way. Essentially what you are doing when you are attempting to read somebody is actually read the emotional cues they are giving away. The physiological changes the body produces naturally, unconsciously and automatically which is almost impossible to mask. Whether that is getting flush in the face when you are embarrassed or perspiring when you are nervous. Trying to control the volume and tonality of your voice when you are angry or fidgety movements of your body when you are anxious, it's very difficult to do.

These physiological responses were once highly useful as they were the only means for us to communicate what we were thinking or feeling. They are still very relevant even in today's world of modern speech with regards to conveying emotion. But where this may work in your favor when building a connection and rapport, it can equally work against a person when they are trying to conceal something.

People in general like to lie, manipulate and deceive, even if it's to a very small degree. It's incredibly difficult to mask the emotional "tells" which go along with these behaviors. So in the following chapters I will lay out exactly what to look for in any situation in order to give you the upper hand in deciphering exactly what another person is really thinking.

I have also included a chapter within the bonus section of this book which helps people deal with interpreting their own emotions, which can go along way in realizing why others are also behaving in the way they are. As I have already suggested, this process has to initially start with you. Become great at knowing yourself, and you will have no problems analyzing others.

CHAPTER 2

A WINDOW TO THE SOUL

"Body Language is a very powerful tool. We had body language
before we had speech, and apparently, 80% of what you
understand in a conversation is read through the body,
not the words"

(Deborah Bull)

So why is it important to be able to analyze people accurately? In
reality it is something successful people naturally do anyway. They
just ensure they hone these skills into something more refined, into
strategies they can put into practical use in everyday settings. For
when you are attempting to build harmonious relationships with
others.

But first, it's a good idea to define exactly what analyzing others
entails. What successfully reading somebody actually looks like. As
we will see shortly, most of what we are reading within the other
person is actually their body language (as opposed to the spoken
words). This is why I focus more heavily on these principles. But
what exactly does body language analysis consist of?

It is essentially the study of everything which is being said outside of the spoken words, the intangibles so to speak. This will include everything in the non-verbal communication spectrum such as facial expressions, body posture, arm/hand/head gestures, handshakes and any and every physical movement of the body large or small.

Then following on from the observation of these variables, the real benefit comes from interpreting and understanding what they mean, what the true underlying feelings and intentions of the person really are. This is especially interesting when it comes to human interaction.

So for the purpose of this book, the terms body language and non-verbal communication will be used to describe the same thing as they are largely interchangeable with one another. People will argue the exact figures with regards to the percentages of relevance in relation to verbal vs. non-verbal communication.

For instance, do you include eye movement (known as oculesics)? What about the depth and rhythm of breathing or the level of perspiration? As I mentioned above, I am personally including all of these variables outside of the spoken words which also includes the tonality and intonation (paralinguistic's) of the voice.

It has been suggested that all of this can equate to as much as 93% of the overall communication value, when in reality this cannot be truly measured as it is entirely dependent on your own definition of body language itself.

I have mentioned this within previous books, but this figure is somewhat of a common misrepresentation from Albert Mehrabian's communication research theory, which was primarily focused on interactions with heavy emotional and "feeling" elements to them, as opposed to normal everyday situations.

Mehrabian who is currently a professor of psychology at UCLA is somewhat of a grandfather of modern body language study and non-verbal communication theory due to his work on the subject through the mid to late 1900's. The figures people most often quote come from two papers he published in 1967 which found that around:

- 7% of the message pertaining to the feelings and emotions of an interaction, come from the actual word(s) which are spoken.

- 38% comes from the paralinguistic element I.e. the way in which the words are said.

- 55% coming from the facial expressions.

So regardless of your exact definition or interpretation of what body language entails, it is safe to say that it heavily influences any and every interaction. It is an agreed upon fact that communication in general is anywhere between 50-90% non-verbal in nature with that figure climbing to the upper end of the range when it comes to more emotional discourse.

The types of interactions you might find yourself in with family members or critical business settings. In fact any face-to-face or one-to-one meeting under any degree of pressure, including first impressions, will heavily involve a high amount of scrutiny and analysis of others. Whether you are aware of it or not.

So remember that your non-verbal behavior will also be being observed during these interactions. However it will be the person who has the greatest conscious control over their movements and gestures who will have the biggest advantage. So make sure you heighten your awareness for these factors wherever possible.

Analyzing others in reality, allows you to gauge so much more about a person and how they are likely to behave in the future. You will be able to much more readily decide if you would like to work with them going forward. So pick up on these factors as much as you can, as they can have such a positive payoff on your decisions.

CHAPTER 3

UNDERSTANDING CUES - CONTEXT IS KING

So having looked at what body language is in a base sense, it's now time to study and identify some of the main components that comprise of this non-verbal framework. This is a reasonably important step in the process in order to give you some context about a situation before critically assessing the meaning behind any specific body language movement or gesture. You need to ensure you are interpreting things through the correct lens.

However the rules aren't hard and fast here. Is a person clenching their hands and folding their arms because they feel threatened? Or are they feeling discontented or perhaps just cold? The answer to this will depend on a variance of factors which you will need to successfully appraise beforehand. So here are the five main contextual factors to pay attention to, to hopefully help you do just that.

Cues

Essentially when humans act, it's very seldom done in isolation. We do things in response to others doing things as part of a sequence or "'loop" of behaviors which feed into one another. A cue simply refers to the initial action or stimuli produced by the environment or other person which will intern elicit or "trigger" a certain response from within us.

If you observe a particular body movement or gesture from another person, this will be the initial cue to start interpreting why they are showing us what they are. These gestures will also start to give away what they may be thinking or feeling to produce that expression or posture in the first place.

These cues will almost always be subconscious emotional reactions to either the outside stimulus or the internal feeling concerning it. As we have seen already with regards to the limbic system, these reactions will be instinctive and difficult to suppress. If a person has just been given some bad news they maybe hunched over with their head down. The action will usually inadvertently give away the cue by its very nature. You can reverse engineer their thought process in the vast majority of cases.

Changes

I will go into the specifics of this principle in greater detail in following chapters but something very important to observe in others is the transitions in their movements, where their body language changes. This might be from a predominantly open stance to a more closed and defensive posture. From a standing position with arms by the side to retreating to a seated position with arms and/or legs crossed.

Something will have initiated this change and it's your job to identify the cue responsible for it. Does the person now feel more threatened? Or perhaps they are trying to conceal something? Are they now looking away, which might indicate that they are being dishonest or even lying to you?

This may work both ways, I.e. in a positive or negative sense. Sales people will watch for these changes which can often just be subtle gestures to indicate if a person is either warming up to what they are saying, and therefore its time to move onto the next stage of closing. Or a regression in body language to signal a step back in the process, and a need to further qualify the customer and get them back onside.

I picked up on these things very quickly in my early business career as I was fortunate enough to have a mentor who would point them out for me. Regardless of what they might be, these transitions can be very significant and therefore very important to pick up on.

Clusters

Similar to the concept of behaviors occurring within a sequence, body language transitions and changes rarely happen in isolation, but rather in clusters. When analyzed more closely they will happen in groups of movements as opposed to a standalone gesture which usually ensures they are easier to identify.

Humans are pattern seekers by very nature so this should come somewhat naturally to everyone. But really honing in on these clusters of gestures can really give you a better idea of what the other person is feeling and thinking.

That being said, there are instances where a simple flicker of an eye lid is all you have to go off. However in most cases people will typically go through a range of movements which are far easier to spot, and tend to provide a much more reliable indicator when translating these movements into the potential feelings and meaning behind them.

For instance returning to the example above, a person may go from initially standing with their hands in a neutral position to sitting down, leaning back, arms folded with a frowning facial expression. Something has now obviously changed, and the sequence or "cluster" of movements will be enough to clearly indicate this.

In reality, when a person does this, they are often times attempting to subconsciously signal what they are thinking. They aren't trying to be deceitful here. Whether it's consciously done or not, these overt changes in movement are usually intentional displays of a persons displeasure or joy, if done in the reverse. As I mentioned previously, a lot of our natural body language was the only means of communicating before modern day speech, so the idea wasn't to hide it at all.

However not all of these cluster movements are so easy to follow. They can be mixed signals and contradictory in nature. A scratching of the head or neck combined with a smile seemingly say's two different things. 1) That the person is potentially being deceitful and attempting to conceal something 2) Additionally portraying an open sign of endearment and affection.

Or is the smile a nervous one which in fact vindicates the first assumption? This is where your analyzing skills and experience will come into play. The following chapters are designed to help you with just that.

Character/Culture

Another factor to take into consideration when assessing the behavior and body language of others is the overall character of the person in question. But also the culture in which they were raised in. This will obviously be greatly dependent on how well you know the individual, and how familiar you are with their conversing and interaction habits.

Is the person more extroverted by nature and likely to display larger and more overt gestures naturally? If this is the case then some of their gestures and movements can be discounted and considered less significance, as this is their baseline behavior. I had a specific college friend who would literally never stop talking. She would almost shout every sentence in addition to this. This was simply her default demeanor.

Conversely, the introverted individuals among us usually express more subtle and concise body language gestures and shouldn't be analyzed as being unhappy necessarily, but rather just a consequence of their default behavior.

You can obviously still watch out for the changes in these people as something done out of character can be a clear giveaway to a change in feeling and emotion. This is likely due to a result of some environmental or internal cue. So try to analyze the people you are observing through the lens of their individual personality traits, and adjust your thinking accordingly.

A similar consideration should be made regarding the individual's background and culture. I have had the opportunity to travel to almost every continent, and I can assure you that whilst the base needs of humans remain the same (as Maslow's Pyramid shows us) the way in which people express themselves can certainly differ.

If a western person were to walk down a busy market street in Dubai, Doha or Damascus, they would be forgiven for thinking that everybody was full scale arguing with one another. Similar to my college friend who used a similar interaction style in her conversations! It would seem hostile, when in fact this is the default way most Middle Eastern populations converse.

On the other hand, if you were to sit a business meeting in Asia, especially Japan or Singapore, you would be forgiven for thinking that everyone in the room is being dismissive or potentially even rude. However this is in fact their default conversational style, and is much more indirect in nature.

The final consideration is that of somebody's age and gender relative to the body language behavior they are likely to display. More pronounced and energetic gestures made by teenage males can somewhat be discounted as business as usual. As once more, it's their default behavior for the most part. Likewise, more conservative and less pronounced gestures and modest postures of elderly women will serve as their baseline reading, as opposed to an inherent assumption of unease or distress.

In general I would say women actually have a better overall perception and ability to analyze others compared to their male counterparts. This is thought to be at least in part due to the evolutionary need to more reliably assess potentially threatening behavior from others, especially larger males, in order to protect their offspring. This may not be the case so much today, however women definitely still retain this ability to interpret body language signals to great effect.

In addition to having a greater innate ability to read others, females also have a higher propensity for more empathetic behaviors which was once again an evolutionary legacy in order to attract

& retain partners and offspring. Empathetic personality types in general will be able to more accurately pick up on body language subtleties, so you are at an advantage if this is you.

Of course shorter term situational factors, such as mood and temperament will also play a part in someones actions within all of the scenarios described previously, so this is not a cut and dry strategy by any stretch of the imagination. But it is certainly wise to take all of these variables into consideration when assessing a persons potential intentions behind their behavior, so you can better analyze them as a result.

Context

Finally, there is one other variable to take into consideration when assessing the behavior and body language of others, and that is the broader context to which the current situation is occurring. Similar to judging the character of others when it comes to analyzing others, we will all interpret these factors based on our own personal contexts.

However in general you need to assess exactly what is happening within the environment you find yourself in. If you are in more of a business setting, people's postures and gestures are naturally more likely to be upright and serious. Conversely, they will naturally be more open and loose within relaxed social settings.

This may seem like stating the obvious. But often times these wider contextual factors will give away the underlying reason for a person's current body language. So do not discount them in the slightest.

The five factors I have explained within this chapter should be considered as overarching principles more than anything. Variables to take into consideration when assessing the body language and analyzing others. They are a compass and preparation step to set the tone and provide guidance for the specific and individual scenarios, which you will find yourself in within everyday situations.

You have to take these factors into account and modify your filters for assessment accordingly. That's not to say you should lean too heavily on them or become closed minded to new information about a situation. They are a crutch for analysis and nothing more. However do ensure you read over these principles once more to give yourself the proper grounding before moving onto the more practical steps which follow.

PART 2: GAINING GREATER SOCIAL INFLUENCE - PRACTICAL STRATEGIES TO SPEED READ ANYONE

CHAPTER 4

WORDS - A GATEWAY TO THE MIND

"Language is to the mind more than light is to the eye"

(William Gibson)

So having discussed the notion that body language is typically the main and determining factor when it comes to successfully analyzing others, it would be beneficial to take a brief step back in the process. To begin with assessing the thing which most people can more easily relate too when attempting to read another persons personality, and that is the words they are speaking.

The spoken word is certainly not everything, as we will see later on, a person can be saying one thing with their words, but quite another with their movements and gestures. But you have to start somewhere. Of course the person could clearly be lying, and again we will also describe strategies to detect this later on. But for the most part, the way in which you can initially decipher what a person is feeling and thinking, will simply be down to the words and sentence structure they choose to use.

Although the brain is an incredibly complex piece of cognitive machinery, when it comes to thought, we think much more rudimentary than most people would believe. To begin with anyway. Most people aren't aware of this, but the thoughts which arise in their mind initially only comes in the form of verbs and nouns I.e. the words used to describe an action and the base context for it.

For example "He jumped" consisting of "He" the pronoun which illustrates the subject and "Jumped" the verb which describes the action. It's not until we translate these thoughts into spoken word or written language do we add the adjectives and adverbs to really describe what we are thinking.

Anything added to this base sentence structure will modify (amplify/deamplify) the quality of the subject and describing words. This is were you can really begin to analyze people as the modifications they choose to make to these sentence structures are voluntary. This will provide big clues into what is going on in the persons mind.

For instance the phrase "He swiftly jumped" gives you an indication into the urgency of the action, but not yet a reason for this behavior. The person may have had to quickly jump as they tried to intercept a pass on the basketball court for example. A fearful person might swiftly jump at the sign of even the smallest animal or insect. Conversely, they may swiftly jump in front of oncoming traffic to save a dog from being hit.

People will include these adjectives to describe and modify a noun, in this case "swiftly" for countless different reasons. However, there will always be a specific reason for their choice. Again, it's here that you can start to interpret what they might be thinking.

So with regards to putting these observations into practice, here are some examples to get yourself thinking along the lines of another persons thought patterns. I like these strategies as they are very unintrusive in there implementation. There is very little probing or questioning needed. Just a simple observation of the words and sentence structure the other person is choosing to use.

1. I persisted until I reached my goal

The signifying word here is "persisted" which suggest the person values the importance of working hard. They strove particularly long with regards to this specific task, much more than they previously might have.

I touched upon the importance of delaying gratification in other books, but this person is showing acknowledgment for this concept. They are portraying this favorable characteristic within themselves suggesting they are a good candidate to work with.

2. I received another pay rise

The signifying word here is "another" which implies the person has already received a pay rise in the recent past or some other form of remuneration benefit, and is now also acquiring an additional one on top of that.

This person is conveying a sense of importance for money and perhaps status. They are also likely trying to reinforce their self-image and in need of adulation from others to feed into their self-esteem. This person will almost certainly respond well to ego-enhancing comments and flattery.

3. I went down the right path

The signifying word here is "right" which counter to the example above, conveys a sense of moral well-being and righteousness. The person is demonstrating that they have an accurate moral compass and can make the correct decisions when faced with important ones.

This is a beneficial behavioral trait for the most part, and demonstrates maturity and a strength of character in general. A person such as this should be praised for doing so.

4. I sat patiently through the meeting

The signifying word here is "patiently" which could imply a number of hypotheses about the persons thinking. The first implication is that of impatience, that the person gets bored rather easily which suggests a negative personalty trait.

The second assumption is the opposite. Although the meeting

wasn't of any particular importance to them, the individual sat through its entirety due to politeness and good manners. Regardless of which of these options may be true, its clear the person is preoccupied with something else.

But like everything I propose in this book, context will always be the defining factor when analyzing others. So a definitive decision will be made after first considering the character and upbringing the person might have had, as well as the social setting you find yourself in.

5. I decided to go on holiday

The signifying word here is "decided" which suggests that the person contemplated their decision far in advance of their action. This may seem obvious with regards to a holiday, as much planning is required. But this statement is also significant for my impulsive behaviors such as buying some new clothes or playing tennis for instance. It implies that the person is less likely to be impulsive in nature as they have thoroughly thought it through before acting.

It may also imply introvertedness, as introverts are thinkers by and large. They mull over decisions in their minds before doing anything. They prefer to sit alone and consult themselves on all manner of options whilst simultaneously recharging their batteries.

On the flip side of this are the extroverts. These people usually take the opposite approach to decision making. They take their energy from other people and the surrounds they find themselves in. As a result they make much more "off the cuff" and immediate actions in more of a trial and error type fashion.

You can see how much can be concluded from just the simple choice of words, or the absence of them. These are just a few of the daily observations you can make with regards to the choices in vocabulary people will choose to make. They are designed to give you an idea of what you want to be watching out for when interacting with, and analyzing others. So ensure you are beginning to look out for these signifying words in your everyday interactions. You will start to pick up on so much more meaning with regards to what others are saying.

CHAPTER 5

WHY YOU SHOULD JUDGE A BOOK BY IT'S COVER

"If you want to find the truth, do not listen to the words coming to you. Rather see the body language of the speaker. It speaks the fact not audible"

(Bhavesh Chhatbar)

So having reviewed the considerations of the various vocabulary choices we make as humans, and the implications they can have with regards to our true thinking. It's now time to move onto the more practical strategies for reading the people around you with regards to body language.

Words can be controlled reasonably well, but as we have seen from looking at the implications of a primal limbic system within our brains. The physiological movements and changes within the body can be much harder to control and therefore mask. These are the "in the moment" elements, the gestures and motions which will allow you to pick up on a persons true feelings, emotions and intentions as a result.

Society in general has long since suggested that "you should NOT read a book by its cover". I would agree that you should not jump to conclusions too quickly regarding someones behavior, but in reality a persons movements and mannerisms is all you have to go on when it comes down to it. So my intention is to give you the tools to more accurately make these calls when you have to.

Analyzing others is about discerning mood for the most part, if you can accurately pick someone's mood you will often know the meaning or motive behind the way in which they are acting. These tendencies are instinctively interpreted by everyone to some degree. It has been suggested that the human body can produce around 700,000 different individual movements, and when combined together, make body language an infinitely intricate discipline to study. However you need to start somewhere.

The following observations and human analyzing strategies are designed to help you with just that. They are meant to be more of a guide as opposed to a 100% reliable rule book. This is more of a framework or reference which you can modify and perfect over time. It has certainly taken me a number of decades to sharpen my skills in this area.

A number of these behaviors will have obvious meanings, however I have still included them as they can easily be missed if you are not fully focused on spotting them. Often times you may find yourself within a busy or distracting room for instance, which may also impair your ability to identify these factors.

Then there are some more subtle "tells" which you should start to add into your repertoire of non-verbal behavior analysis skill-sets and people reading tool box, as you go along.

As I eluded to earlier, culture and upbringing can have a major impact on the more pronounced and kinesthetic body language movements. However, for the purpose of this book, I have tailored this guide based on the behavior of the Western World by and large. These implications will be catered towards those of the North American and European regions in general. However many of these observations are applicable across the board.

I apologize in advance if some of the things here seem overly obvious or counter to what your own culture would dictate. I would ask you to suspend any preconceived notions whilst you read through these observations and just have a go at implementing a few within your day-to-day life. You may be surprised at the accuracy many of the signals will give you.

The non-verbal cues and behavior tendencies I state from here on out are grouped with regards to specific body parts for ease of analysis, starting from the legs and feet. Then moving onto the arms and hands and finally to the all important gestures and expressions of the head and face.

CHAPTER 6

PATTERN SEEKING SECRETS - LEGS & FEET

After countless years of assessing body language and non-verbal variables for meaning, I have noticed one particular habit that most people will adopt when attempting to analyze others. People will almost always and automatically focus their attention towards the face. This is for good reason as these gestures are some of the most accurate portrayals of thought available to you. As we will see later on, its the subtle movements of the eyes and mouth which give away a person's true intentions so readily.

However, what these people often forget to take into consideration is that the other person is also very much aware of this tendency. They are cognizant of displaying such signals and will be consciously attempting to combat this behavior within themselves. They will be trying to mask it for the most part. As I have mentioned previously, this is easier said than done, but a factor nonetheless.

However it is the lower limbs, the feet and legs which often go unnoticed. This is the reason why you should be paying very close attention to them, all of the time. For hundreds of thousands of years our ancestors were largely only concerned with mastering the art of bipedalism, I.e. mastering the ability to walk and run in an upright position when it came to the legs and feet.

Thankfully this is no longer the case. The world of today has us largely just standing and sitting around, and as a result, we naturally forget about what we are doing with our legs and feet. This is why you need to pay special attention to them. The head and face can be intentionally kept still and devoid of emotion. However, the legs and feet will still move, albeit unconsciously for the most part.

Now of course you will need to take the usual context variables into account when assessing lower limb body language signals. We need to preface this by stating that men and women have tendencies to stand and sit in a different manner from one another which will be in part due to clothing choice, anatomy/physiology and just behavior differences in general.

Men and especially younger men are naturally more inclined to sit in an open stance with knees and legs separated and pointed outwards. This is an overt alpha display as they are exposing the genitals. Women will naturally sit in a more closed position with legs crossed at the knees and pointing to one side. Again, this is in part due to clothing choice if wearing a dress or skirt for instance. But may well be due to cultural influences as much as anything else.

Here are some of the key signals to look out for regarding the lower limbs when attempting to analyze others:

Crossed Vs. Uncrossed

As I have previously mentioned, variances here will differ with regards to gender and also within certain cultures. But for the most part a person sitting with their legs crossed is a show of closed and apprehensive thinking. The person will often be guarding something and you should proceed with some level of caution. It may also infer a degree of disinterest and insecurity.

There are also some subtle differences in the way that people cross their legs. The traditional American leg cross or "figure of 4 leg cross" as it's often phrased, is most common. This is where a person will rest the ankle of one leg on top of the knee of the other, creating a figure of 4 shape with the rest of their body.

This will naturally tend to ensure that the person will lean back which creates the classic professor or therapist seated look you see in movies. I had a post-grad lecturer at Stanford who literally perfected this pose. I would always make a mental note of his posture when I sat appraisal sessions in order to master it myself. But I still haven't quite managed it.

This type of pose will still typically indicate closed thinking and apprehension as their leg is forming a barrier to the body, but it does suggest a slight degree of openness as the crotch is exposed.

This is in slight contrast to the European leg cross which is more conventional, with both knees crossed one on top of the other with both legs firmly closed. If a person is exhibiting this sort of crossing, it tends to indicate a guarded mindset.

Conversely a person sitting with their legs open and uncrossed, is more a sign of general openness in attitude. It can even signal confidence and dominance so watch out for how you approach a person in a situation such as this. But like everything I am suggesting here, make sure you are always taking the wider context into consideration.

Implications of Leg Direction/Pointing

The general rule of thumb with any limbs with regards to the direction in which they are pointing, is the same across the board. If somebody is sitting down they will unconsciously point their legs or knees to an area of interest. If you are speaking with them and they are pointing their legs towards you, it's a sign of attentiveness, interest and openness to what you are saying.

This is an especially relevant and reliable indicator of interest when they have just sat down. The longer the person sits in a position they are likely to adjust themselves randomly to get comfortable again. This renders any subsequent analysis much less significant and useful.

Conversely the opposite is true if they are pointing their legs away from you. You may have to alter your interaction style as you may have lost them somewhere along the line. This rule also applies with crossing of the legs, especially if you are sitting alongside the person shoulder-to-shoulder.

I watch out for this all of the time. I can be opening a conversation with a stranger on the street who is initially very coy about what I'm saying. At some point I will build enough rapport to where they will switch their leg position from being crossed at the knees, and pointing away from me, to pointing towards me. These are the changes I suggest as being so important to pick up upon, as they are so simple to spot.

Much like the knees and legs in general, the direction in which the feet are pointed is usually significant. They are almost always pointed towards an area of interest. Once more, it is a subconscious show of attentiveness and openness to what the other person is doing or saying.

People will commonly align their feet to point towards the leader or alpha within a group, or to someone with a high degree of natural gravitas. People are always looking for strong individuals to follow, so watch out for this foot movement during social gatherings or within a large crowd of any kind. This easy form of analysis can tell you an awful lot.

CHAPTER 7

THE GRAVITY OF GESTURES - ARMS & HANDS

"If language was given to men to conceal their thoughts, then gesture's purpose was to disclose them."

(John Napier)

It's not just the legs and feet which can give strong and suggestive meaning with regards to the way in which they are crossed or direction they are pointed. Many of the general rules here also very much apply to the upper limbs of the hands and arms. Like the legs, arms are a very reliable indicator of mood and intention and are usually somewhat more active as they are under greater conscious control.

This however does indicate that whilst the arms and hands are great non-verbal behavior analysis signals, they can be manipulated and controlled a little more easily compared with the legs. This can sometimes lead to false/positive signals. A person will more commonly realize they are doing something with their hands and arms, compared with the lower limbs, and change this behavior to distract from their true intentions.

In general the arms and hands are a defensive barrier to the body and indicate openness and security when in a neutral position by a person's side . Conversely, apprehension and insecurity are expressed when they are crossed in front of the chest. In fact holding anything in front of the body like a bag or papers for instance will signify this barrier being built.

Again the caveat is always context, these indications are just possibilities and percentages when assessing somebody's thinking, but very well worth taking on board nonetheless. The knack to analyzing others will always be a process of stacking reading skills one on top of another.

So here is a look at the key factors to take into consideration when reading upper limb body language, to give you another layer to work with:

Crossed Vs. Uncrossed

Similar to the legs and feet, crossed arms will usually signify closed and protective behavior. This can be on a scale from general disinterest, and perhaps even boredom, all the way to extreme animosity and hostility. This is especially true if the hands are clenched into fists. You will have to assess the context as always and look for other cues like facial expressions to confirm your assumptions either way. Is the person relaxed and smiling? Or do they have a serious frown on their face?

The other form of crossing is done by holding or clenching the upper arms with the hands whilst the arms are crossed. This is a form of "self-hugging" and can be done with both hands/arms in a more obvious manner or with just the single arm with it being held and clenched by the person's side. This type of behavior is usually a female trait and one they typically exhibit when feeling threatened, or just a general sense of insecurity about a situation.

Conversely open arms in a neutral position either placed in front of the person or down by their sides, will suggest the opposite to the above. It signals that they are not threatened by anything in the immediate environment and even ready to greet and embrace others with a handshake or closer bodily contact. It's the first subtle sign of empathy and openness, so watch out for this when you can.

The final significant signal of an uncrossed arm position to take note of is the hands held behind the back. This is more of a dignitary or military stance and is a clear show of confidence and authority. It indicates that the person is so comfortable with handling themselves and their surroundings that they can afford to position the hands behind them, exposing the torso as they do not fear any attack from the front.

Take note of the people who do this as you will instantly know a lot about their current mindset. Conversely exhibiting this arm position yourself when wanting to appear confident and assured is a intelligent move to make.

So whilst the arms are a very good indicator of feeling and emotion when it comes to analyzing others, the hands specifically are even more so. Similar to aspects of the face, signals given via the hands can be extensive. Hands are extremely expressive and dexterous. This means they can be used in more intricate ways to gesture mood and motive, to a greater extent compared to the larger more cumbersome limbs. But it takes a more trained eye to spot them.

It has been estimated that the hands contain more neural connections to the brain than any other peripheral body part, and for good reason. We use the hands to navigate almost everything in the physical world by touch and can both consciously and unconsciously signal such a wide range of intentions as a result. They are able to give standalone signals with regards to the direction they are pointing or in conjunction with other body parts in the form of holding, clenching, scratching and tapping, just to name a few.

Hands are involved in everything from handshakes when greeting, to waving for goodbyes. Along with the fingers they can make the more obvious expressive signals like the western style "thumbs up" or "OK" sign to indicate contentment or validity of a point being made. They can of course also be used for more crass one and two finger gestures. You can use your imagination here!

However where it really gets interesting with regards to the hands, is where they start to interact with other objects. This might be separate body parts such as a scratch of the nose/ear or fiddling with a cigarette packet or pen. These moments are often known as "leaking signals" as they are indicating a momentary glimpse into what the person is really thinking. Again they might be saying one thing with their words but quite another with their hands.

So here is a breakdown of what the key hand movements and gestures can signal:

Hand Position

When assessing hand posture or position, there is really only two considerations to make when attempting to analyze someone. Two considerations which may allude to the way in which the person is thinking and feeling.

The first of these is when the palms are facing up or open to the rest of the room. This is a signal of submissive behavior generally, it's an appeal to honesty and truthfulness and is thought to stem from the time humans would signal a lack of weaponry or potential harmful object at their disposal. It's a suggestion of innocence or that "I don't know the answer" type of gesture.

This concept also very much applies to the handshake, a fundamental gesture of trust. It is a customary greeting virtually everywhere is the world today, and once again can be traced back to more adversarial type encounters. Ancient Greek texts depicted soldiers shaking hands before battle as early as the 5th century BC.

This behavior can be seen all the way up to the modern Japanese Samurai who not only offered the hand as a gesture of peace, but always with the right hand. This was due to there being no left handed Japanese swordsmen as the energy protecting Ki inscription would always be placed on the right side of the tang by the sword smith, to protect the body from evil spirits when sheathed.

Therefore an offer of the right hand would signal they could not draw the sword from across the body on the left hip. There are a number of other analogies of why it's most customary to shake with the right hand, including that of basic hygiene etc. However the Samurai story is certainly the one I like the most.

If a person offers you their hand with palms facing upwards it's a subtle submissive gesture and one of openness to you. It invites you to place your hand on top of theirs with your palm facing down in a more dominating fashion. However it's actually untrue that you can tell a lot more about someone from their handshake as it's such a common gesture, other than the fact it shows confidence and assurance when done firmly.

It certainly say's more about a person's general thoughts and feelings if they do not offer it. Firmer handshakes can be faked quite easily though, to give the impression of sincerity, so I wouldn't pay so much attention to them other than the fact that you should shake hands firmly at all times yourself. My early business mentor would never speak to anyone he knew without first shaking their hand, looking the person directly in the eye before addressing them by their first and last name. I've never seen anybody get so much out of everyday interactions than this guy.

Alternatively a show of the hands being turned downwards, with the palms hiding from view in a more closed position, signals the opposite. It's more a show of strength, authority and possibly even dominance. Watch out for situations where you are talking to somebody and their hands are firmly and obviously placed downwards in front of them on a table or desk for instance. They will certainly need some work to open up and may indeed by hiding something in addition to just their palms.

CHAPTER 8

HIGHEST QUALITY "TELLS" - FACIAL EXPRESSIONS

The previous two chapters were designed to give you a grounding in the typical body language considerations when it comes to the limbs of the body. These can prove to be very accurate signals when you know what you are looking for. However there is a final layer of study when it comes to analyzing people. The most powerful of all.

If the gestures of the hands and arms were more subtle and under greater conscious control compared with the legs and feet, the movements of the head, mouth and eyes are even more so. During interactions between human beings, over 90% of their gaze is directed towards the other persons face, so any signs given off here, regardless of how minor can be significant.

People intuitively know that the gestures of the head and face are under the most conscious control and attempt to mask them as best they can, which only further builds on the significance when they are spotted. So its time to start paying very close attention.

Head

The head is a very significant part of the human anatomy for obvious reasons. It houses the most important organ in the body for cognition and nervous system control, therefore exhibits some very powerful defensive and self protective movements. In general the head will actually lead the rest of the body with its movements for the most part. It will be the driver for all other subsequent body language.

It is also closely connected with the facial features and these signals are often given in conjunction with one another. The difficulty in spotting some of the smaller movements and gestures will be offset by the proximity of the features I.e. the head & face is a small enough surface area to pick up on even the slightest signals as they occur.

Due to the flexible and dynamic nature of the head via the connection with the musculature of the neck, it can elicit a wide range of oscillating and rotation motions/gestures. This will include simple agreement or disagreement nodding and shaking, all the way up to more lateral head tilting. This tilting action can have a few meanings depending on the angle and direction of the tilt, but again is reliant on the context of the situation in relation to the facial gestures which accompany it.

A slight and slow tilt to either side with an intuitive gaze is often viewed as a submissive signal. It indicates interest and curiosity in what the person is saying. It also suggests a level of trust as the person is exposing the throat and neck, which also makes them appear smaller and more vulnerable. However a tilt of the head backwards tends to suggest a feeling of suspicion, distrust and uncertainty, especially if combined with congruent facial expressions exhibiting the same. It's a more defensive movement, a subconscious rocking back of the head to remove it from danger.

Other than these stated tilting expressions, considerations with regards to the head can be reasonably obvious, such as speed and range of motion I.e. faster and more pronounced movements signaling a greater conviction and intensity to ones thought (in agreement or disagreement). Conversely slower and smaller nodes and shakes will convey the opposite in the persons thinking.

One tip for whenever you are trying to appear calm and confident or even attempting to conceal something yourself, is to make sure your own head movement is minimal. Keep it in a still, upright position whilst speaking clearly. Truly confident people exhibit very little head movement in truth. My mentor would always look straight at you and speak with perfect posture and statue like poise. It was somewhat memorizing, and it would ensure I was entirely focused on exactly what he was saying.

Mouth

The mouth is unquestionably an integral part of human communication, but not simply due to the fact that in combination with the larynx (voice box) we can produce sound and modern day speech. The mouth also gives off very important cues with regards to analyzing people, especially when the other person is not talking.

Speech and oration are thought to be great conveyors of message, but it is also a great way to conceal what a person is thinking. The very action of talking will often over power and mask any subconscious gestures the mouth will be making, when the person is listening for instance.

Similar to the considerations of the hands, the mouth has many moving parts and can display a whole host on gestures which signify a great range of meaning. Unlike the nose and ears, which are typically only brought into play by the hands when assessing body language, the mouth acts independently to a large degree and therefore requires greater and more detailed analysis.

One of the most obvious considerations is that of the smile. When assessing somebody's sentiment when they are interacting with you, one of the biggest giveaways of insincerity is a false smile. A genuine smile will be performed in unison with the rest of the facial features. All facial muscles will contract including those of the cheekbones and most importantly those around the eyes.

If a person is smiling only with the mouth, you should immediately question what they are thinking. This faking of a smile may also be done by dropping the jaw or with a "twisted" type smile which is uneven on both sides. Both of these unnatural movements of the mouth also typically suggest the smile is forced, and therefore the person is potentially concealing true feeling.

Another signal which is worth mentioning is the act of biting the lip or grinding of the teeth. Both of these motions suggest an element of tension, frustration or even suppression of emotion. They are general displays of unease and should always be given credence when noticed. In fact I am always wary of a person who cannot control their mouth movement and keep it still when they are not talking.

This goes along the same lines as excessive tapping of the fingers or playing with a pen. As we will see later on when discussing the deceptions signals, movement masks feelings. Everything from biting of the lip, excessive smoking, chewing of gum and even talking are typically used to keep the mouth busy in order to prevent it from signaling frustration and deception tells.

So while stating that the mouth acts independently as a body language signal compared to the nose and ears, there is one traditional exception. The biggest and most obvious way to tell if a person is apprehensive or even being deceptive is excessive touching of the mouth and specifically biting of the nails. I don't need to point out the significance of this to you, if the person is unable to keep two of the most consciously controlled and important body parts still I.e. the hands and mouth, at the same time, something is definitely up.

Eyes

I have reserved the observations regarding the eyes till last when it comes to analyzing others. These thought pattern and emotional cue giveaways can be such an important factor and tool in this process. So much so that many body language experts prefer to leave the study of the eyes, in respect to analyzing others, to a separate discipline altogether known as oculesics.

Whilst I do believe the eyes deserve special and individual consideration due to their accuracy in discerning intention, I always include them as part of the overall process of reading a person in general.

Eyes are what we predominantly use to assess the world around us, but it works both ways. Not only do we use them to look outward into the world, it has long been stated that looking into the eyes of another person can tell you a great deal about their internal thoughts and feelings.

"The eyes are the windows to the soul"

(William Shakespeare)

Eyes are simply mesmerizing by their very nature and play a large role when it comes to hypnosis techniques. Even making strong eye contact with a stranger on the street can feel like a significant event. However with regards to reading and analyzing others, we are actually more concerned with eye movement more than anything. To say the direction in which the gaze changes in relation to the behavior of others and questioning of them.

The following observations are intended to help you with just that, to give you any idea of what people are really thinking regarding their eye movement. For the sake of these descriptions "left" and "right" side are in relation to the individual, and not the observer.

Looking Left or Right

So in general a person will predominantly look to one side when being asked a question. They will either look left or right when reflecting, recalling or remembering information. The side in which they look relates to the side of the brain they are accessing for the most part. The right hand side being largely concerned with creativity, emotions and feeling, whilst the left hand side deals with the facts, figures and memory.

Now this is broadly speaking of course, and there are other intricacies and nuances we will explore below. But in a general sense, assessing eye gaze and direction can be a very accurate indicator into someone's true thoughts and feelings. Overall if a person is looking to the right it indicates that they are creating something in their mind, they are tapping into the creative centers of the brain in an attempt to fabricate, guess and story tell.

This obviously isn't an issue if you are asking them a question and they respond by looking right and saying something like "I'm not really sure, but I imagine it would be like this". They are genuinely being honest here by giving you an impression of how they think it would be, and not stating they know it for sure.

However if they look right and say something like "I was in that situation last week and this is how it played out". This is more worrying as they are stating something as an affirmative, something they know to be true from a past experience and memory. However when responding they were accessing the creative/story telling part of the brain whilst they did it. This is not to say they are definitely lying, but it is a big red flag nonetheless.

To really assess these observations more accurately, you need to pay attention to whether the person is also looking up or down whilst looking to one side. In relation to the above example, if the person is looking downwards and to the right, this would indicate they are accessing the creative areas within the brain, but more closely related to emotion. They may just be recounting the feelings they had regarding the situation they are being asked about, as opposed to actually fabricating the answer.

However if they are looking upwards whilst also looking right, this is more sinister as this would indicate that they are fully accessing the imagination centers of the brain and heavily suggests that they are indeed fabricating whatever response they are making.

Conversely looking left when answering such a question would signify they were genuinely accessing memory centers and are telling the truth. This is especially true if the person is looking upwards and to the left which indicates recollection from the memory and image centers of the brain, greatly implying truthfulness in what they are saying. Similarly looking downwards and to the left also indicates honesty as it's a cue for recounting self-talk and rationalization about a given situation or subject.

So make sure you are paying very close attention to someone's eye movements the next time you are interacting or asking questions of them. These movements can be small and subtle, but can give so much away in terms of the persons true thoughts and intentions.

I was fascinated with the study of oculesics during my final year a Stanford. I would analyze literally everyone I came into contact with. I certainly felt it gave me an advantage when heading into business life too. Feeling out the true intentions of prospect clients and employees can save you so much time and money in the long run.

General Eye Contact

The only other important observation to make with regards to the eyes and there movements, is direct eye contact itself. I have already suggested how it can be a powerful and mesmerizing thing, and will also say a lot about someone's personality, especially when they are speaking or listening to you.

This will carry greater significance compared with moments of reflection, after being asked a question for example. When eye movement can vary due to factors such as recollecting or imagining information, which I have described above. However when talking or listening, strong eye contact always indicates honesty and sincerity with the occasional instance of nervousness, where it can be discounted.

So this concludes the considerations with regards to the analysis signals of the head and face. Certainly do not ignore the other body parts we have already discussed as they certainly have merits in their own right. However make sure you are always paying special attention to the gestures of the head and face, as they can have such significance when you do spot them.

CHAPTER 9

DECEPTION DETECTORS

"The most important thing in communication is to hear what isn't being said"

(Peter Drucker)

So having gone through the various elements of body language analysis when it comes the analyzing people in general, it's now time to identify some of the specific signals which could in fact imply deception. Signals which are unintentionally or designed to throw you off track.

Whether people would like to admit it or not, this is really what a person is after when they are attempting to learn how to read the thoughts, feelings and intentions of others. They want to know if the other person is telling the truth or not? They would like to avoid being taking advantage of wherever they can, which is why this advice is so popular.

Similar to the preceding chapters, I will go through the following examples in order of body part. Starting from the lower limbs, the legs and feet. Then moving onto the arms and hands, before finishing with the all important gestures of the facial features.

Warning Signs

Legs & Feet

As I have also previously stated, movements of the lower limbs can very often be unconscious motions as we tend to think much less about what we are doing with them. In particular it would be wise to watch out for fidgety feet at all times. People can mask the emotions of the face, but will often release this tension with the feet.

Watch out for excessive tapping or moving as it is the biggest sign of impatience, nervousness and possibly even deception. If the head, face and voice are saying one thing but the feet are saying another, give president to the latter.

Arms & Hands

In general, analysis of the hands with regards to reading intentions can get extremely interesting when they start to interact with other objects or body parts. This is usually done in an attempt to cover up some momentary conflict or dissonance within the person's mind. A disconnect from what they are saying and what they are in fact thinking.

The first and most obvious sign of this is hand interaction with the nose. It is no secret that the face and nose can start to flush with blood when someone starts to feel anxious or nervous when not telling the truth. Touching or scratching the nose is often an unconscious act of trying to hide this change of color.

This can range from minor embellishment and fabrication to full scale lying. The old children's fable of Pinocchio, the wooden boy whose nose grew every time he told a lie is very apt here, and shows that the nose has long been synonymous with not telling the truth. Its actually called the 'Pinocchio Principle' when taught to psychology students.

Similarly to this, if somebody is pinching their nose whilst listening to others speaking, can also suggest the person is holding back information or perhaps stalling on giving a response. This is especially true if they are also covering the mouth at the same time. Kids will do this overtly and unapologetically. They will cover their mouth with the palm of their hand to signify that they have a thought in their mind, but do not want to say it out loud. This seems to have developed into a more subtle and subconscious act in adults.

These deception signals are not confined to the nose either, they can equally be exhibited by touching and scratching of the ear/head/neck. Essentially what a person is doing is compensating for the internal irritation they are feeling regarding the lie they are telling with an outside physical gesture to mask it. The one caveat here is that these signals can also be triggered by common and genuine nervousness, especially if the person is not confident with public speaking for example.

However for the times when you are in more relaxed and comfortable settings, always watch out for these subtle hand cues or "tells" when you suspect someone is trying to cover something up, or be untruthful with what they are saying. This will obviously overlap heavily with eye movement and other facial expressions which we will move onto next.

Finally, along with watching out for fidgety feet, you also need to do the same with arms and hands at all times. Now it's a little less of a significant tell compared to the feet, as the hands are under greater conscious control. But once more, you need to watch out for excessive tapping of the fingers or scratching or the arms, neck or face which can simply be an indication of impatience or nervousness, but possibly a sign of deception.

Facial Expressions

I have already covered the potential implications of a false and untrustworthy smile in a previous chapter. It is something which can be picked up upon quite naturally by most people as there will be a clear and distinct difference in the signals given-off by the eyes and mouth by and large. The mouth maybe smiling, but the eyes will not be.

I have also described the implications the various eye movements will have on potentially deceitful statements made by people. So make sure you go over the information in practice on everyone you come across. The only other truly significant and consistent "tell" you can rely on when it comes to deception detectors for the facial expressions, is blinking of the eyes.

Like every other body part, watch out for erratic behavior and excessive movement of the eyes. The eyes should blink between 5-15 times a minute, and anything over 20 times should be viewed as abnormal and suspicious (unless they obviously have some momentary irritation of course).

SUMMARY

Successfully analyzing others can be a vast and complex area of study, and a seemingly daunting pursuit for one to take on if you do not know what you are looking for. However it really is just about breaking down the various elements before putting them back together to complete the behavior puzzle. To build the picture of what somebody is really thinking.

You have to start with yourself, the reason why humans act the way we do to begin with. You have to look at both the physiology and psychology behind behavior. In our case, these traits are deep rooted in our evolutionary journey. Back to a time when modern speech wasn't an available tool for us, a time when non-verbal gestures were the name of the game when it came to signaling our thoughts, feelings and emotions.

The question for us today is simply how much of this ancestral legacy do we still hold onto? The answer is certainly a substantial amount, and that is largely due to our limbic system or our "old mammalian brain". Regardless of how much we have developed as individuals or civilization and society have in general, we still cannot fully escape the influence these primitive brain structures have over us.

Analyzing people is really only about reading the signals these sub-conscious systems are setting off. As I have already mentioned, they stem from a time when non-verbal gestures and cues were the only mode of communication we had, and therefore are extremely difficult for us to mask.

However we do still learn a lot from our environment. Larger more conscious movements and mannerisms of the limbs can be cultur-ally rooted. That is why it's important to assess the contextual cues first and foremost. This starts with assessing the cues which are likely to trigger off certain behavioral traits. These can be both external and internal, but will always be the subsequent driver of the proceeding behavior.

The next thing to watch out for is the changes, the sequences of signals which allow you to more easily pick up on mood. Large shifts in body language displays will almost always occur in clusters or in a grouping of mannerisms, allowing you to much more reli-ably pick up on these changes when they do occur.

The fourth consideration is regarding the character and culture of the individual or group of people you are assessing. As I mention, the subconscious cues are almost always the same within everyone, but the larger and more overt body movements and gestures can be very much interpersonal, depending on somebody's upbring-ing and background. Try to assess for their baseline behavior and make adjustments to your thinking either way.

Context can play a huge role in accurately assessing the momentary behavior of others, and credence should certainly be given to the situational settings you find yourself in. Discount any contextual etiquette within formal and business settings for instance. These factors shouldn't be the only lens by which you are assessing somebody's intention with regards to their body language, but considerations that would be wise to take on board nonetheless.

However analyzing people isn't just about mannerisms and gestures. You do still have to pay attention to the words these people are choosing to use. Care must be taken here as language can be a great mask for intention. However you can still deduce a great deal about a persons mindset if you know what you are looking for within their vocabulary.

This will come down to the adjectives and describing words the person chooses to use. The emphasis they place on the base nouns and verbs within their sentences to accentuate meaning. This will show much about their current mindset.

Only then can you start to move onto analyzing the specific parts of the body when reading a person, to truly assess the thinking behind their behavior. This starts with the lower limbs, the legs and feet. People often neglect to pick up on the signals from these body parts as they wrongly presume that they do not hold much weight.

However this is untrue, as the signals given via the legs and feet give very significant signs. They are under much less conscious control and often go unnoticed. So can give very genuine signals as a result, so should not be dismissed. Subconscious crossing and/ or pointing of the knees and legs will say a lot about a person's attentiveness and mood.

The same can be said of the arms and hands in terms of crossing and general direction. However due to the more intricate and expressive ways in which they can be controlled, the arms, and especially the hands can give an even greater range of non-verbal gestures.

Make sure that you give special attention to the interaction the hands make with other body parts, such as those of the head and face. Gestures given as a standalone can be very powerful cues, however when they are performed in conjunction with others, that signal amplifies even more so.

Most people typically only concentrate on facial features and head movements when it comes to analyzing others, and I can see why. These signals are of high significance, even compared with the arms and hands. The facial features are almost always in sight and under the most conscious control compared with any other body part. Hence special effort is usually given in an attempt to not give anything away here, people even practice their "poker face" in the mirror.

This brings us onto the specific deception detectors. The signals which potentially give away untruthful behavior. These "tells" regarding the face, only have to be minor. A flushing of the face or flicker of the eyebrow often enough to suggest a hidden agenda.

Also watch out for the interactions of the hands with the nose/ears and mouth. Touching of any one of these areas will signify something. It may just be a genuine momentary bout of nerves, or maybe something more sinister the person is attempting to mask. But as always, make sure you watch out for excess movement and fidgeting from any body part, be it the hands, feet or eye lids. If there is one "tell" which signifies general unease and possible deception most accurately, it is this.

CONCLUSION

Analyzing people is not an exact science. It's more of an art form in truth. We all read people to a certain degree naturally, but there are certainly specific signals and cues to better guide this process. You need patience and to develop your skills for spotting these tendencies over time. It's often a game of percentages. What does this signal mean most of the time? It's about assessing the myriad of the contextual questions about a situation, and then reaching your conclusions from the information available.

Although the words and phrases people are using do need to be taken into consideration. Body language plays a much larger role when analyzing others. This is why I have focused more heavily on these principles within this book. This is especially relevant when you are sensing a level of untruthfulness in the other person, when you are suspecting deception perhaps.

Recent studies have shown that strangers will lie 3 times on average within the first 10 minutes of meeting one another. However not everything said here is an attempt to be deceitful or dishonest. Often times we are simply abbreviating what we are saying for ease of explanation. Or telling a small white lie to protect the other persons feelings. "Do these jeans make me look fat?" You get the picture.

Of course on the whole, I believe its better to be as honest and forthcoming as possible. But human interaction is filled with areas of gray. My intentions for this book was to give you a better idea of how to navigate this uncertainty. To decipher what other people are really thinking by way of their actions, from the body language they are portraying. Then you can deduce from this, what you will.

It is now up to you to put these principles into practice yourself!

I wish you the very best of luck.

BONUS CHAPTER

(From 'Emotional Intelligence: A Psychologist's Guide')

CHAPTER 4

TAKING INVENTORY OF YOUR EMOTIONAL STATE

"Educating the mind without educating the heart is
no education at all"

(Aristotle)

One of the most important things you can do when initially starting out on your emotional intelligence enhancing journey is to take stock of what you are currently feeling. There is no right or wrong answers here in terms of what come up. As our limbic legacy show us, humans are inherently emotional creatures and suppressing them is almost impossible to do entirely.

However you do have control over the way you react to these tendencies, the thoughts and behaviors after the fact. The following factors should help you take a closer look into how to identify and deal with these feelings when they do arise to ultimately move you to the next level in your E.Q. journey.

Acknowledge Your Emotions

The first thing to do when attempting to increase your personal E.Q. levels is to get good at acknowledging and perceiving the emotions that you are feeling. This is the starting point for every model and framework of E.Q.

Whenever I feel an emotion arise within me I always take a pause and acknowledge its presence, I take a moment and really feel it so I can understand and label it in my mind. This isn't the same as reacting or acting upon the emotion just yet, but I want to know why it may have arisen and if it could be useful to me. If it's a feeling of anger, fear or frustration I do not deny or try to hide it, but instead acknowledge its presence and dismiss it as not being productive and move on.

If you start to dwell on emotions such as these you will quickly fall into a negative spiral thought process that will have you framing everything in a pessimistic light before you know it. I used to play out entire imaginary scenarios in my head of something going badly and the knock-on effects that I 'knew' it would have, only to realize that it NEVER worked out that badly and that I'd fabricated it all in my mind. Sound familiar?

If on the other hand it is an emotion of excitement, joy or anticipation, I also pause for a moment, acknowledge and label what it is that I'm feeling and try to cultivate and utilize it if I think it will benefit the situation such as situational empathy (which we will get onto later).

It is also important to take responsibility for these emotions that you are feeling either way, good or bad. Know that it is something inside of you which is eliciting such a response and that you have to deal with it and not sweep it under the carpet so to speak. This is usually the most challenging step for people, but it is also the most rewarding. Yes it maybe some outside influence or stimulus that sparked the response in the first place, but remember that the emotions you are feeling are coming from within you and that it's your responsibility to deal with them

Understand That You Are Not Your Emotions

So following on from that, you also need to constantly remind yourself that the emotions which arise within you and the conscious entity which interprets them are two very different things. Most people walk around in somewhat of a waking sleep for the most part completely at the mercy of any feeling, thought or emotion that pops into their head.

You have to understand that many thoughts and emotions will pass through you almost on a second by second basis, but again it's entirely your choice on how you perceive and choose to react to them.

There is also a very large egoic element to this process as well. Thoughts and feelings of jealously for another person or fear of performing a task is really just your ego trying to keep your preconceived notions about the world intact and keep you operating within your comfort zone. This is a topic for much greater discussion i.e. regarding the tactics to counteract such self-sabotaging behavior, but needless to say that detaching yourself from your overall emotional state is very a beneficial thing to do.

Learn to Forgive Yourself & Others

"Life becomes easier when you learn to accept an apology you never got"

(Robert Brault)

Again, along the same lines as letting go of a negative emotion that arises within you, people have a great tendency to hold onto what they perceive to be negative acts that they have either committed themselves or others against them. Holding onto this ill feeling again serves absolutely no purpose to you in the immediate future and certainly not the long run. *"Holding onto anger is like drinking poison and expecting the other person to die"* as the Buddha so aptly put it.

If there was one thing that got me ahead in my business life so quickly it was this concept. Once I stopped getting caught up with what I thought I deserved from a situation or others around me and started pushing ahead regardless, I made so much more progress. You can't stop and throw stones at every dog that barks, and that includes yourself when you mess up.

This isn't just applicable to adult and business life either, it's relates to everyone young or old. If I had taken heed of this advice when I was growing up I know I would have had better overall relationships with school/college friends and family alike. That's not to say things were necessarily that bad, but they could have been better, or at least I could have saved myself a great deal of heart ache and stress along the way.

Don't Get Involved in Negative Self-Talk

As I mentioned above, letting negative self talk get out of hand is a very bad habit to take up. I would say that it is the one thing that plagues humanity more than anything. We often talk ourselves out of things before we've had a chance to start them. Again this comes down to letting negative thoughts and emotions cloud our thinking to a point of almost no escape. You have to stop this in its tracks as quickly as possible if you want to build high overall levels of emotional intelligence.

This also includes negative self-talk and 'gossip' regarding other people. In danger of sounding like one of your parents or school teachers here, you don't need me to tell you this is a worthless exercise and one that will ultimately bring your E.Q. level down with it. No one is perfect; just make a point of catching yourself when you start to talk in this way.

Also along the same lines as the above, you must try and do your best not to judge others where ever possible. This actually freed me greatly in a psychological sense when I managed to stop doing it a few years ago. I never thought of myself as an overly judgmental person but I still realized I would do it from time to time. But stopping myself altogether from judging anyone I came across in even the smallest way saves me so much mental energy and almost certain daily miss judgment.

Nowadays I simply let others go about their day in their own way without even the slightest judging thought about their behavior. That is not to say that I tolerate bad behavior or that I do not try and empathize with people and attempt to understand their situation better, which is critical to building fruitful relationships. But I don't judge them with regards to how they got to where they are, I never walked in their shoes or went through the struggles they did so I let them do the talking on this one.

Again this isn't some "holier than thou" situation, I'm not perfect and do very occasionally catch myself automatically judging someone. I just now catch it very early and stop myself in my tracks straight away. It's so much more liberating when you do.

BONUS CHAPTER

(From 'NLP: A Psychologist's Guide')

CHAPTER 7

LOOP BREAKS & PATTERN INTERRUPTS

The brain is undoubtedly an extremely complex organ within the human body. It is required to perform an incredible number of calculations every second even during mundane tasks like guiding the various parts of the body for movement in simple motor skills all the way to making crucial and complex decisions in real time. The brain undertakes millions of these interconnected decisions every single day thereby making it one of the most powerful pieces of biological machinery we have.

However we still do not fully understand the extent of it's complexity and inner workings. One thing we do know is that the brain is solely responsible for enabling people to develop thought patterns and habits that ultimately dictate not only their daily behaviors but also their thinking patterns. It does this in an attempt to optimize a person's day-to-day movements and thought processes, but these short cuts aren't always beneficial.

In order to form these "loops" or "patterns" the brain undertakes several processes that help it both develop a certain habit and make it a part of routine life. In this segment, we will start by taking a brief look at the meaning of cognition in general, which is fairly critical when it comes to NLP. Cognition is simply the study of how the brain perceives information and represents it within the persons mind. It tells us how the brain functions and helps in putting that information to use.

The branch of study that deals with establishing a relationship between learning and cognition is known as neuropsychology, an area of study I once specialized in myself. Neurology has intrigued scientists for as long as the concept has been around with many psychologists having studied its intricacies for decades now. Right from classical conditioning described by Pavlov and John Watson to the operant conditioning of B F Skinner, each one presented theories that described how the human brain works and learns.

It is no secret that a person's daily habits and thinking routines will ultimately dictate how productive and successful they are. However habits are impartial, they will either help a person attain their desired results and remain persistent in pursuing them. Or they will ensure they continue getting the average/poor results they have always gotten. As Dr Bandler pointed out "Brains aren't designed to get results; they just go in directions".

In terms of general behavior it is usually just a case of learning your ABC's so to speak i.e. learning the sequence of the Antecedent, Behavior and Consequence. This concept was originally based on Skinner's model of cognition, antecedent, behavior and consequence being the three main steps involved in developing a habit. In a nutshell they are described as follows:

Antecedents

Antecedents are stimuli that precede a behavior or reaction. They are situations and circumstances that cause a person to behave in a certain manner. Antecedents determine the outcome of a certain behavior by inducing it automatically.

In simpler terms, antecedents are people and situations that solicit a certain reaction or behavior. They are what lay down the basis for habits, they hold the key to how a person reacts to any given situation.

Antecedents are studied to know whether the reaction is a result of positive reinforcement or punishment by and large. Having this knowledge makes it easier to predict future behavior. It is fairly simple to manipulate antecedents in order to evoke the desired behavior.

Behavior

The second component within the habit development model is behavior. Behavior is the response provided to the stimulus. It is meant to serve two main purposes namely to get something that a person desires or to avoid getting something they do not.

It is important to note that almost all behavior is learned from significant others. Some is reactionary but all is observable and measurable.

This means that behavior is both visible to others and is a reflection of the person's mind. For example, if a person is angry then their behavior will come through in the form of a changed facial expression or an angry physical reaction. This behavior differs from person to person and is not constant, but rather based on their learned behavior through observing others during past experiences.

As I mention, behavior is also measurable. This means that it is possible for another person to describe the behavior after observation. For example, a person can observe another person getting angry and describe his reaction. This behavior can be altered to give away a desirable outcome.

Consequence

Consequence is the final component and is a result of the behavior phase. It can be viewed as the environment's reaction to a certain behavior. A consequence will be a direct result of the behavioral action. For example, if a person reacts to a certain situation in a negative manner then the consequence is bound to be negative. Say a person slams a vase on the floor out of anger then it is obvious that the vase will break and the person will have to clean it up.

Consequence is also measurable just like behavior.

Basically if you are fully aware of the process I described above you can alter it for your own benefit. It involves understanding the cues, following a routine and availing the consequence/reward. The key here is to aim for the desired results but change the antecedent and rewards, then the behavior will automatically change accordingly.

For example, if you are trying to learn a new skill, but buying books in order to achieve this is not inspiring you enough to study the material then changing over to online classes may inspire you to better effect.

Similarly, you also can change the reward in order to modify the behavior. For example, when trying to excel in a competitive exam, you can look forward to treating yourself to a toy/clothes you have wanted to buy for a long time. Both can work as a motivating factor for you to modify the behavior enough.

The above method works great for changing more general behavioral patterns I find. However we are more concerned with the thinking habits here as opposed to just the behavioral, although they somewhat go hand in hand. That is what real NLP seeks to accomplish. For that you need to view things in a slightly different way, to adopt another approach.

TOTE Process

With regards to the thinking process in NLP there is a similar structure that the mind follows. It's sometimes described as the path of least resistance approach and is made up of four components the Trigger, Operation, Test and Exit. I'll elaborate on each in a little more detail below:

Trigger

Similar to the ABC sequence of behavior learning I described above, the TOTE process starts with an antecedent or cue known here as the trigger. In NLP it's also called the 'Anchor' from time to time and once again relates to the impetus or stimulus which starts off the pattern.

Operation

The operation once again like the ABC process, relates to the behavior portion of the pattern and the thinking habit that we undertake.

Test

However this time the mind performs a 'test' of that preceding behavior to identify whether the intended outcome was met or not. Did the person get the desired result from that action? If the answer is 'no', then the person will continue through with the behavior cycle until they do.

Exit

If the answer was 'yes' to the test stage, then a person will simply move on with their behavior and proceed to close this thinking pattern loop so to speak. This completion stage must happen in order to not continually go round in circles.

This is how we typically form habits in thinking which can be very powerful cycles especially if built and reinforced over a long period of time. It isn't necessarily a bad thing if this thinking loop is genuinely a beneficial one, but if it is not then it can be quite destructive. We can see this quite clearly in individuals with high obsessive compulsive tendencies (OCD).

In any case these cycles can be reasonably difficult to break but it's imperative that you do in order to move on from a negative cycle. That is one of the main tenants of NLP, breaking these negative thought patterns to replace with better and more beneficial ones. This process certainly played a critical role to my overall success. When I really learnt how to pattern interrupt.

Thought Pattern Interrupt

The idea is to disrupt a negative thought pattern as early on in the cycle/sequence as possible, more specifically between the trigger and the operation. Regardless it must be completed before the testing phase of the condition, to say that you must disrupt it before the mind tries to test the original operation pattern otherwise any attempt to break the sequence will be of little use as the pattern is almost completed.

The pattern interrupts aren't that difficult to implement and it is simply about stopping your train of thought and thinking about something different, butting in on your own thought process/ conversation you are having within your own head.

Like Richard Bandler suggests, we are simply trying to change the direction of the mind and reprogram it as we do. You are not removing the old pattern per se, but rather redirecting around it.

Go big!

The idea is to make this interrupt as big and bold as possible. If there is one mistake I see from people who try this method is that they are too weak with their disrupting action and it isn't enough to fully divert their thinking. Especially if it is a long term entrenched habit of thought they are trying to break.

Try a loud clap of the hands or loud cough. If the cycle which is trying to be broken is a negative thought process with depressive emotions attached to it, then try breaking the pattern with a little dance/jig or a laugh. Try to inject humor into the disrupt as it is completely counter to the original and unwanted behavior and congruent with the newer, happier thought process.

Timing is Everything

As I described above, timing is everything here. You need to ensure you catch the trigger phase as accurately as you can as it will be key to identifying when you need to employ the pattern disrupt. In essence this should be directly after and as soon as possible following on from when the trigger is spotted.

However in reality this is likely to be a very short period of time so you really have to be a keen observant throughout the day to catch them when they do occur. For me it was usually some thought or memory which popped into my head that would start the cycle, especially the negative ones.

If I let it continue my emotions and physiology would start to change when in it would be too late. I have now learnt to catch this right before this transition takes place i.e right after the trigger thought/memory and replace my momentary operation/behavior to a more positive one.

Rinse & Repeat

However that is simply not enough in my experience, just catching the cycle once. The real payoff comes from repeating this cycle over and over until the new behavior pattern becomes habitual and you start to see the results you are looking for.

So make sure you perform whatever interrupt you have chosen until it becomes second nature to you, until you no longer have to think about it. You have to bring the skill into the "Unconscious Competence" phase when performing it. That is when the new direction of thought and subsequent behavior will really take hold.

This general approach was taken from hypnotherapists such as Milton Erickson who used pattern interrupts to disrupt the waking thinking patterns of their participants. They would lead a persons inner monologue down a familiar path before disrupting the line of questioning leaving the persons unconscious mind waiting for the logical next step of the pattern to occur, but it never comes. This can be a powerful enough confusion of the mind which puts a certain percentage of the population into a hypnotic trance.

You are not attempting to go that far with yourself, and it's almost impossible to do it on your own. But the general thought pattern interrupt is designed to work along the same lines. But this time to disrupt a familiar negative thought pattern and replace with a positive and more beneficial one.

Made in the USA
Lexington, KY
31 July 2018